SCIENCE KIDS

Big
and
Small

Aaron Carr

Go to **www.av2books.com**, and enter this book's unique code.

BOOK CODE

L 8 0 1 0 9 3

AV² by Weigl brings you media enhanced books that support active learning.

AV² provides enriched content that supplements and complements this book. Weigl's AV² books strive to create inspired learning and engage young minds in a total learning experience.

Your AV² Media Enhanced books come alive with...

Audio
Listen to sections of the book read aloud.

Video
Watch informative video clips.

Embedded Weblinks
Gain additional information for research.

Try This!
Complete activities and hands-on experiments.

Key Words
Study vocabulary, and complete a matching word activity.

Quizzes
Test your knowledge.

Slide Show
View images and captions, and prepare a presentation.

... and much, much more!

Published by AV² by Weigl
350 5th Avenue, 59th Floor New York, NY 10118
Website: www.av2books.com www.weigl.com

Library of Congress Cataloging-in-Publication Data
Carr, Aaron.
Big and small / Aaron Carr.
    p. cm. -- (Science kids)
ISBN 978-1-61690-943-7 (hardcover : alk. paper) -- ISBN 978-1-61690-589-7 (online)
1. Polarity--Juvenile literature. 2. Form perception--Juvenile literature. I. Title.
BF293.C37 2012
153.7'52--dc23
                      2011023415
Printed in the United States of America in North Mankato, Minnesota
1 2 3 4 5 6 7 8 9 0 15 14 13 12 11

062011
WEP030611

Project Coordinator: Aaron Carr   Art Director: Terry Paulhus

Weigl acknowledges Getty Images, iStock, and Dreamstime as image suppliers for this title.

Big
and
Small

CONTENTS

3

Big

The hippo is big.

Bigger

The elephant is bigger.

Biggest

The whale is the biggest.

Small

The mouse is small.

Smaller

The goldfish is smaller.

13

Smallest

The bee is the smallest.

Big

The lion is big.

16

Small

The meerkat is small.

Bigger

The polar bear is bigger than the fox.

18

Smaller
**The fox is smaller
than the polar bear.**

Biggest

Bigger

The whale is the biggest.

Big

Small

Smaller

Smallest

The bee is the smallest.

21

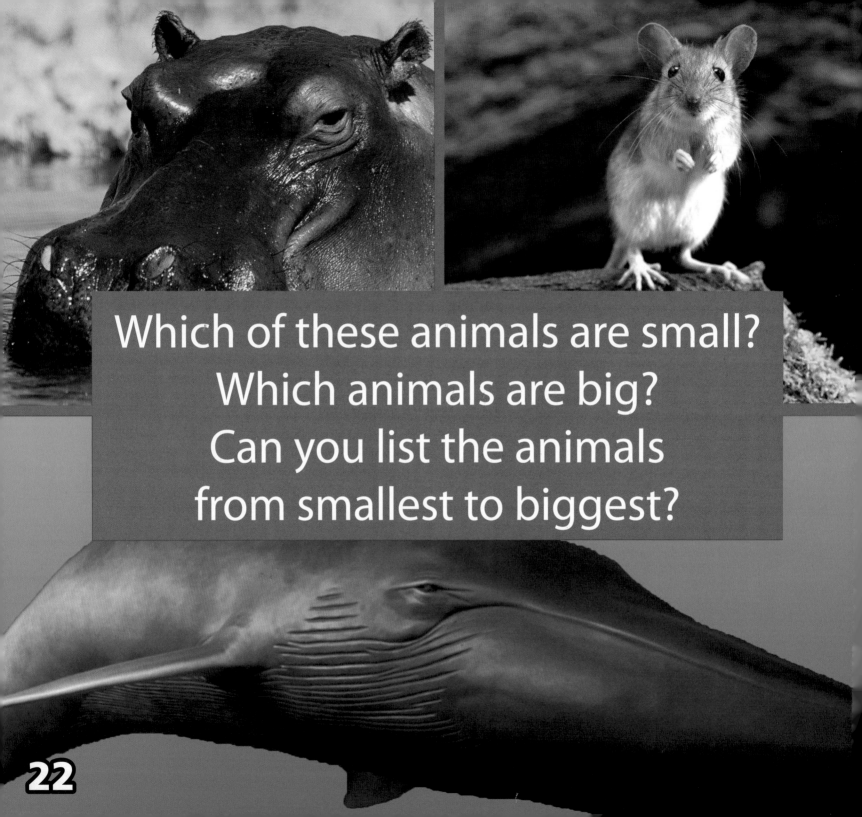

Which of these animals are small?
Which animals are big?
Can you list the animals
from smallest to biggest?

22

WORD LIST

Research has shown that as much as 65 percent of all written material published in English is made up of 300 words. These 300 words cannot be taught using pictures or learned by sounding them out. They must be recognized by sight. This book contains 15 common sight words to help young readers improve their reading fluency and comprehension. This book also teaches young readers several important content words. These words are paired with pictures to aid in learning and improve understanding.

Sight Words		
animals	is	the
are	list	these
big	of	to
can	small	which
from	than	you

Page	Content Words First Appearance
5	hippo
7	elephant
9	whale
11	mouse
13	goldfish
15	bee
16	lion
17	meerkat
18	polar bear
19	fox

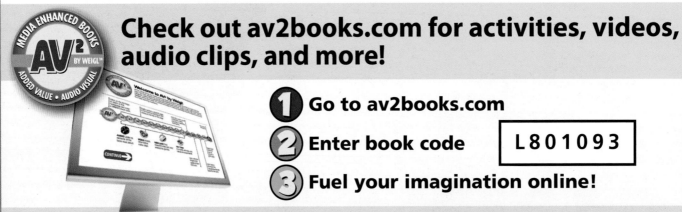